FOREWORD:

WHAT CAN I [illegible] ABOUT GRANT PARKER
THAT HASN'T ALREADY BEEN WRITTEN...
AND WHAT CAN I SAY ABOUT BILL RECHIN
AND DON WILDER THAT HASN'T BEEN SAID.

TO FIND OUT: TAKE EXIT 16 ON THE TACONIC
PARKWAY NORTH AND STOP AT THE FIRST
COMFORT FACILITY.

ONCE INSIDE, ENTER THE DOOR MARKED
"ROOSTERS", AND READ THE WALL IN
THE THIRD STALL TO THE LEFT.

IF YOU ARE AN EMPLOYEE, PLEASE WASH
OUT YOUR MIND BEFORE LEAVING.
IF THIS IS AN INCONVENIENCE TO YOU,
JUST READ THE BOOK... IT'S PROBABLY
BETTER.

JOHNNY HART

D0627257

PROPERTY OF
COLLIE LANNUM
735 0801

I HATE MONDAYS

by Parker, Rechin and Wilder

A FAWCETT GOLD MEDAL BOOK • NEW YORK

I HATE MONDAYS

© 1976, 1977, 1978 Field Enterprises, Inc.

© 1978 CBS Publications, the Consumer Publishing Division of CBS Inc.
All rights reserved

A Fawcett Gold Medal Book published by arrangement with Field Newspaper Syndicate.

ISBN: 0-449-13978-6

Printed in the United States of America

10 9 8 7 6 5 4 3 2 1

BONG!!

ONG-ONG-ONG-ONG,
ONG-ONG-ONG-ONG,
ONG-ONG-ONG,
ONG-ONG-ONG
Bill Rechin

DO ME A FAVOR, MERLE....
...STOP LEAVING OUR NAMES AT THE WAKE-UP DESK.

tuesday

wednesday

I GOTTA GET OUT.... I'M STARVING!

HERE OL' BUDDY... ..I SPENT TEN YEARS CARVING THIS...
Bill Rechin

CHOMP CHOMP CHEW CHEW CHOMP CHEW CHOMP
...NEEDS MORE SALT.

thursday

WHAT'S THE ENEMY'S NUMBER?

I JUST SCOUT 'EM, I DON'T DATE 'EM.
Bill Tochin

friday

THIS MONOTONY IS DRIVING ME NUTS.
WHAT'S MONOTONY MEAN?

DOING SOMETHING THAT'S MONOTONOUS
WHAT DOES MONOTONOUS MEAN?
Bill Tidwell

IF I'VE TOLD YOU ONCE I'VE TOLD YOU A MILLION TIMES.

saturday

WILL I EVER RUN THE 200-METER HURDLES AGAIN, DOC?

SOON AS WE GET THAT NASTY OL' CANNON BALL OUT OF YOU, CALVIN.

WHAT'S MY CHANCES?

NOT BAD... IF WE'RE LUCKY IN OUR EXPLORATORY SURGERY.

THE DAY IS MINE, CROCK!

YOU'VE THROWN EVERYTHING YOU GOT AGAINST ME!

THUNK
...MAN, THAT PORCELAIN SMARTS...
Bill Tidwell

tuesday

Z
THEY'RE ALL ASLEEP...
CRAWL CRAWL

...PASS THE WORD.

...HOW DO I PASS THE WORD WITH NO COMMUNICATIONS SYSTEM?

..BY WORD OF NOSE.
Bill Rechin

wednesday

HOW'S THE EQUAL RIGHTS MOVEMENT GOING, ROSIE?
JUST FINE, FREDDY...

...WE GOT EQUAL PAY, EQUAL BENNIES.... EVERYTHING WILL BE EQUAL NOW.

NEED ANY OFFICE HELP?
WITH THOSE LEGS?

thursday

....OH MIGHTY NEBOOCANEZZER... I AM CURSED WITH TEN PROBLEMS OF WOE..THERE IS FEAR AMONG MY PEOPLE.. ...CRIME AND CORRUPTION RUNS RAMPANT... DROUGHT THREATENS TO DESTROY...

YOUR THREE MINUTES ARE UP... DEPOSIT ANOTHER FIFTY CENTS.
I, AIN'T GOT NO CHANGE!

..THEN YOU GOT ELEVEN PROBLEMS OF WOE, CLYDE.
Bill Tidwell

friday

DWAINE TWAIN HAS DESERTED AND JUMPED INTO THE WELL AGAIN, SIR.

FISH HIM OUT!

WE TRIED BUT HE'S NOT BITING THIS MORNING.
Bill Tenkin

saturday

Bill Tackin

THAT WAS TAKEN THE DAY I LEFT HOME.
WHAT A BRAVE SMILE.

SHE'S PROBABLY THE TYPE THAT HIDES HER FEELINGS.

YEAH... SHE WANTED TO DO BACKFLIPS.

tuesday

WHO'S THAT POOR DEVIL?
JULES SCHEMEESE, THE FAMOUS....
READY..
..AIM..

...TROUBLE MAKER
PUNCH
PUNCH
PUNCH
HIT
HIT
HIT
Bill Tidwin

PRETTY BOY CAPTURED POULET AND WANTS TO MAKE A PRISONER EXCHANGE.

WE HAVEN'T GOT ANY PRISONERS.

...HE'LL TAKE TWO FIRST ROUND DRAFT PICKS.

thursday

YOU'LL ENJOY THIS BOOK, ...IT'S A BOOK WITH A MESSAGE.
WHAT'S THE TITLE?

IT SPANS A GENERATION OF READERS...IT'S MORE THAN JUST A BOOK
WHAT'S THE TITLE?

...THOUGHTFUL AND DISTURBING IN SCOPE....A BOOK YOU WON'T SOON FORGET.
IT'S A DIRTY BOOK

friday

WHERE'S POULET?

HE'S ATTENDING LEADERSHIP SCHOOL, SIR.

...THAT'S LIKE SENDING MICKEY MOUSE TO M.I.T.

saturday

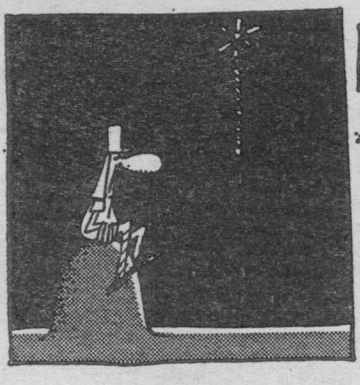

PLOOK!

monday

GET RID OF THESE WILD ONIONS!

COM'ERE FRED... I GOT A JOB FOR YOU...

...NO WONDER I STRIKE OUT AT THE SINGLES BAR EVERY OX!! NIGHT.
'CHOMP' 'CHEW' CHEW'
Ric Tochini

tuesday

SCUFF
SCUFF
SCUFF
SCUFF
SCUFF..
SCUFF..
SCUF

SCUFF..
SCUFF...
SCUFF...
.....SCUFF..

WHERE'S THE COMMANDANT BEEN?
...TAKING HIS EVENING SCUFF

ALL WE GOT LEFT IS A BITE OF CHEESE AND A GULP OF WATER...IF WE'RE CAREFUL...

GULP!
WHO DRANK OUR LAST DROP OF WATER?

I DID... CHEESE ALWAYS LEAVES A LOUSY TASTE IN MY MOUTH

thursday

WHAT LIES AHEAD, STRANGER?

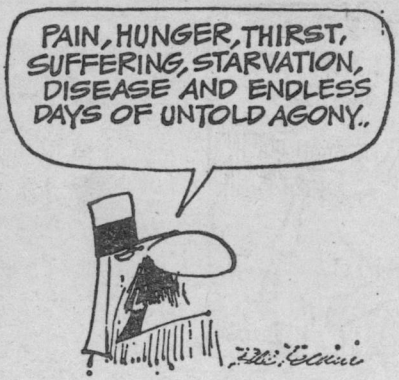
PAIN, HUNGER, THIRST, SUFFERING, STARVATION, DISEASE AND ENDLESS DAYS OF UNTOLD AGONY..

...HOWEVER, IF YOU DECIDE NOT TO STOP AT THE FORT...

friday

CHARGE THIS MAN WITH DISCRIMINATION!
SERIOUS CHARGE, POULET...I'LL NEED PROOF.

THESE WERE FOUND ON HIM.
LOTS OF MEN OWN DOMINOES

WHITE WITH BLACK DOTS?
Bob Tinelli

saturday

YOU BEEN DOWN IN THAT WELL EVER SINCE YOU DESERTED?
TWENTY-THREE YEARS THIS JUNE.

YOU MUST HAVE A MILLION THINGS BOTTLED UP INSIDE OF YOU...GNAWING AT YOUR GUTS...

...BEGGING TO BE HEARD.

MIC-KEY M-O-U-S-E

tuesday

...TOMORROW I DO BATTLE WITH THAT DEVIL, CROCK.. WHAT IS YOUR ADVICE, WISE ONE?

"DON'T WHITE UNTIL YOU SEE THE SHOOT OF THEIR EYES."

YOU LOONEY LUMP OF LIMESTONE!
..WORDS AND BONES MAY STICK MY STONES, BUT...

wednesday

CLEAN OUT THE GOAT PEN, IRWIN

...DO YOU REALIZE I'M A COLLEGE GRADUATE?

OH... I'M SORRY.

CLEAN OUT THE GOAT PEN, IRWIN

thursday

WHAT ARE YOU THINKIN' ABOUT, JESSIE?

BUNNIES.

AIN'T YOU NEVER GONNA GROW UP?
Bill Watterson

friday

HOW'S OUR WATER HOLDIN' OUT?

HOW YOU HOLDIN' OUT, WATER?

...I'M SUFFERING FROM NASAL CONJESTION, SNIFFLES AND MINOR SORE THROAT.

NOT SO GOOD.

saturday

SIR, WE'VE GOT TO STOP. ....THE MEN CAN'T SEE A THING.

ARE YOU ABSOLUTELY SURE?
YESSIR.

...THEN SERVE SUPPER.

monday

SMALL, INSIGNIFICANT SANDSTORM APPROACHING!

...AT TIMES BECOMING HEAVY.

tuesday

THIS IS YOUR COMMANDANT SPEAKING..
YES SIR!
YESSIR!
YES SIR!

...DUE TO THE PRESENT SANDSTORM CRISIS.....

...I'M UNABLE TO SEE YOUR FACES.
YESSIR, FISHFACE!
YESSIR, BUZZARD BOD!..
YESSIR, NOZZEL NOSE!
Bill Tacline

wednesday

DRASTIC MEASURES MUST BE TAKEN, POULET..
...THE SITUATION IS CRITICAL!

YOU MIGHT BE OVERREACTING, SIR.....GET A SECOND OPINION FROM FIGOWITZ.

I'M STANDING ON FIGOWITZ.

thursday

HOW WE GONNA LOCATE THE PRISONERS?
NO PROBLEM, SIR.

TEN-SHUN!

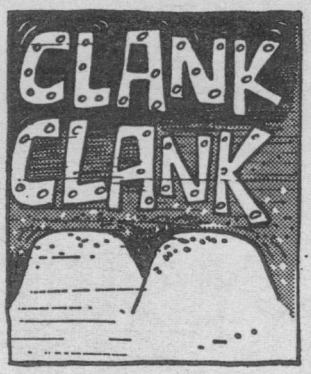
CLANK
CLANK

..THE LAST TWO BUMPS ON THE LEFT.

friday

LOUSY @&!!#* SAND!

...MORNING, MAG... LOVELY DAY, ISN'T IT?...
SPLAT

THE GOOBER PEAS COULD USE A LITTLE MORE SALT.

saturday

SSSHHHHH

...IT'S STOPPED! THE SANDSTORM'S GONE!

SOMEHOW I LIKED IT BETTER WITH THE SAND.

HIYA BABYCAKE... YOU BUSY TONIGHT?
HUBBA..... HUBBA.. YOU TURN ME ON LIKE GANGBUSTERS.
WHISTLE WHISTLE

CAN'T A YOUNG GIRL WALK PAST YOU BEASTS WITHOUT HEARING SUCH ABUSE?
Bill Tidwell

tuesday

WE GOT TWO CHANCES OF GETTING BACK... NONE AND ZILCH

LET'S VOTE ON IT.
Bill Rechin

wednesday

WHAT'RE YOU DOING?
I'M WRITING A REPORT ON THE ALARMING INCREASE IN OFFICE THEFTS.

...I'D LIKE YOUR OPINION

WHERE'S PAGE THREE AND FOUR?
Bill Watterson

thursday

LUNCH TIME!

WHAT GOES GOOD WITH A CHEVY FUEL PUMP, ...CHIANTI OR CHABLIS?

friday

874... 875...876.. 877.....
WHAT ARE YOU DOING?

I'M COUNTING THE STICKERS ON THE CACTUS.
THAT'S A STUPID THING TO DO.

YOU ONLY GO AROUND ONCE.
Bill Watterson

saturday

WE GO THAT WAY!
YOUR SENSE OF DIRECTION IS AMAZING!

...MERELY A MATTER OF REMEMBERING A FEW BASICS...
...FOR EXAMPLE, THE SUN ALWAYS SETS IN THE WEST...

...EXCEPT FOR THE MONTHS BEGINNING WITH "R".

monday

tuesday

CRAWL...
CRAWL...
CRAWL...
CRAWL...

WHAT DID YOU FIND OUT?

HOW FAST ONE'S NAVEL FILLS UP WITH SAND.

YOU KNOW... LIFE AIN'T SO BAD IF YOU THINK OF EACH DAY AS AN EXCITING AND PROVOCATIVE ADVENTURE.

LIFE AIN'T NUTHIN' BUT ONE, BIG, DULL CLICHÉ!

I DISAGREE... BUT THAT'S WHAT MAKES HORSE RACES.

thursday

WAIT'LL YOU SINK YOUR CHOPPERS INTO THIS DISH....

I'M ENTERING IT IN THE NATIONAL BAKE-OFF!

PLOP

THERE GOES MY WEEK OF "FUN IN THE SUN" IN BEAUTIFUL DOWNTOWN SCRANTON.

CLANK

I JUST REALIZED SOMETHING, BILLY JOE
WHAT'S THAT?

..I'M NOT ALL BARK
Bill Teitelbaum

saturday

CRAWL
CRAWL
CRAWL...
CRAWL...
WHAT ARE THEY UP TO?

..THEY'RE SLEEPING... NOT A CREATURE IS STIRRING, NOT EVEN A MOUSE.
YOU SURE?

YOU DON'T OVERLOOK A "STIRRING MOUSE" IN THIS BUSINESS AND LIVE TO TELL ABOUT IT.
Bill Tallon

KNOCK KNOCK KNOCK KNOCK
CANDY MAN HERE!

BOOM!

HOW WAS I TO KNOW CHOCOLATE-COVERED GOOBERS BREAK YOU OUT?

tuesday

GOOD MORNING, LITTLE BLUEBIRD OF HAPPINESS.
WHAT'S WRONG WITH YOUR LEG, LITTLE BLUEBIRD?
Bill Watterson
I SLIPPED GETTING OUT OF THE GX!IX BIRDBATH.

wednesday

YOU WILL LEAD THE STRIKE FORCE IN TOMORROW'S ASSAULT ON DUNE NINETEEN.

...THIS WILL DEMAND LIGHTNING-QUICK DECISIONS, PLUS THE MOST SOPHISTICATED WEAPONS AND TECHNOLOGY.

I GET THE PICTURE, SIR....

...WILL WE BE SHIRTS OR SKINS?
Bill Tekin

thursday

EVERY TIME YOU PLAY THAT THING, I THINK OF GROSSIE.

THAT SONG DOES IT, EH?

NOT THE SONG ...THE SHAPE.

*!!@
#!@*!!
!!....

..*@! CRUMMY JOB....*!@
STINKIN' HEAT...@*! FLIES
...LOUSY HOURS.....*#
... ROTTEN PAY!...

WHY DON'T YOU QUIT?

...AND LOSE MY KEY TO THE EXECUTIVE RESTROOM?

saturday

YOU REMIND ME OF CALVIN WERTENBAKER.

PUNCH
POUND
POUND
POUND

...YOU KNOW CALVIN?

GOOD MORNING, LITTLE BLUEBIRD OF HAPPINESS.

YOU GOTTA BE KIDDIN', CLYDE... MY SISTER AND HER FOUR KIDS ARE UP FOR THE SUMMER, THE IRS. IS AUDITING MY RETURN AND MY TWO KIDS GOTTA HAVE BRACES.
GUESS YOU DON'T FEEL LIKE SINGING ONE LITTLE CHORUS FROM...

CHOMP

GUESS NOT

tuesday

POOR HORNBLOWER WON'T MAKE IT... HOW ABOUT A SMILE AND A WORD OF CHEER?

NO PROBLEM, DOC... ...I'M A GREAT PICKER-UPPER!
Bill Rubin

HI THERE, GONER.

THE LAST TWENTY YEARS MUSTA BEEN TOUGH FOR YOU, DWAINE.
DESERTING AIN'T BAD... I GOT MY GUPPIES TO KEEP ME COMPANY.

WHERE'S THE BIG FELLA?
OBEDIENCE SCHOOL... HE GETS HOME AT FIVE...

...GOT HOME AT THREE 'TIL THEY STARTED BUSING HIM.

thursday

PLOP
NOW WHAT.. PERKINS?

(GASP)....PRETTY BOY'S MOB JUMPED ME AND CAPTAIN POULET DURING CANNON PRACTICE.....

DID POULET STAND COURAGEOUSLY BY YOUR SIDE?

....YOU EVER SEE A WHEELIE DONE ON A FOUR-HUNDRED POUND CANNON?

friday

JULES SCHEMEESE... YOU ARE CHARGED WITH RUNNING CROCK'S CAT UP THE FLAGPOLE.....

..PUTTING WOOLY WORMS IN THE GOOBER PEAS AND DUNKING POULET'S SKIVVIES IN CHICKEN FAT.
....ANY LAST WORDS?

I'LL NEED A LAMPSHADE.
Eric Teubul

saturday

I GOT THIRTY-FOUR ON MY I.Q. TEST.

...I'M NOT A BIT SURPRISED

ME NEITHER... THINGS ALWAYS COME EASY WITH ME.

...AM I LATE?

YOU IDIOT! ..YOU MISSED THE FIGHT!

WILL THERE BE A MAKE-UP BATTLE NEXT WEEK?
Bill Rechin

tuesday

POOR OL' DIRON....

...CROCK CAUGHT HIM STEALING GOATS... HUNG HIM BY HIS EARS FOR NINE MONTHS, THEN SENT HIM TO THE SALT FLATS.
YEAH... I REMEMBER HIM... BIG, UGLY GUY.
Bill Rechin

SHHHH.... HE'LL HEAR YOU.

..LOAD CANNON!
...LOAD CANNON

ONE CUP POWDER
...ONE CUP POWDER

...AND A PINCH
THIS AIN'T BAKE DAY, JABUL!

thursday

I'M STARVING, WALTER... LET'S STOP FOR A SNACK.
I KNOW JUST THE SPOT, EDNA..

... 31 GREAT FLAVORS TO CHOOSE FROM.

LOSING FOURTEEN MEN ON PATROL BOTHERING YOU, POULET?

IF ONLY I HAD IT TO DO OVER AGAIN.
Bill Tidwell

WE CAN'T SPARE TWENTY-EIGHT MEN.

saturday

YOU A GOOD SWIMMER?
MOMMIE TAUGHT ME HOW.

.....THREW ME IN THE LAKE WHEN I WAS TWO YEARS OLD.

DID'JA HAVE ANY TROUBLE?

NOT AFTER I GOT OUTTA THE BAG.

THOSE LOUSY SCUM CUT THE WIRES LAST NIGHT.... NOW WHADDA WE GONNA DO?

I'VE HIRED JAQUES LA PIDGE ....THE WORLD'S MOST FEARLESS CARRIER PIGEON.

HE'LL BE ZOOMING IN ANY MINUTE TO SAVE THE FORT.....
Bill Rechin

...LOOK TO THE SKIES!
SLAM

tuesday

PRETTY BOY'S ATTACKING... GET THIS MESSAGE TO HEADQUARTERS.

JAQUES LA PIDGE: YOUR MISSON IS TO FLY THIS MESSAGE THROUGH BLAZING CANNON FIRE TO SAVE THE FORT.
Bill Tackin

YOU'RE OUTTA YOUR BUCKET, CLYDE!

wednesday

..YOU GONNA FLY OUR MESSAGE THROUGH THE SAVAGE FIRE OR AINT YA?
NO WAY, BABY!

YOU LIKE PIGEONBURGERS WITH OR WITHOUT ONIONS?
Bill Rechin

ZEE COMMANDANT HAS FOUND ZEE WAY.

thursday

JAQUES LA PIDGE IS OFF! ...OUR FEARLESS FEATHERED FIGHTER WILL SAVE THE FORT!

..CAREFUL OF THE SAVAGE CANNON FIRE!
Bill Tarbin

SLAM
NICE GOING, BLABBER-MOUTH!

WHADD'YA GET FOR DESERTING UNDER FIRE, LA PIDGE?
NINETY-NINE @*!#!! YEARS!

CLANK
THAT AIN'T SO BAD.

HOW MANY HUNDRED-AND-TWENTY-YEAR-OLD PIGEONS YOU FED POPCORN TO LATELY.. FATFACE?

saturday

STOP YER BELLY-ACHIN', LA PIDGE.
...YOU DESERTED UNDER FIRE!
...TAKE YOUR MEDICINE.
SQWAAK
OK!!
AWK..
SQWAAK
SQWAAK
SQWAAK

NINETY-NINE YEARS IN THIS CRUMMY DUMP! ...I AIN'T GOT ROOM TO BREATHE!

...TAKE THE STATUE OUT.
Bob Tinsley

GOOD MORNING, MEN... I'LL BE YOUR LEADER FOR TODAY'S SAVAGE FIGHTING.

NO WAY!...
WE AIN'T GOT A CHANCE NOW...
...I'M DESERTIN' @X!!#!
WE'RE DOOMED!
SAY YOUR PRAYERS, GANG!
YOU GOTTA BE KIDDIN'

I'LL PRETEND I DIDN'T HEAR THAT.
Bill Watterson

tuesday

DIDJA HEAR ABOUT KRUEGER'S OL' MAN LEAVING HIM A BUNDLE OF DOUGH?
WHAT'S HE GONNA DO WITH THAT KIND OF MONEY?

HE'S GONNA DRIVE UP TO THE GAS STATION AND SAY..."FILL'ER UP"!
THEN WHAT?

WHADDYA MEAN... THEN WHAT?

I think that I shall never see.....a poem as lovely as a.....

.....big toe.
Bill Rechin

thursday

YOU STICKIN' ANYTHING BACK FOR RETIREMENT, MAGGOT?
NAW... I'M GONNA LIVE OFF MY LOOKS.
Bill Griffith

...I WONDER HOW I'D DO LIVIN' OFF MY LOOKS?

...LIKE DARTH VADER WORKING IN A KISSIN' BOOTH.

YOU OUGHTA BE ASHAMED OF YERSELF, SCHEMEESE..THROWING CROCK'S CAT IN THE DRYER.

...HAVE YOU ANY IDEA WHAT YOU PUT THAT POOR CAT THROUGH?

THE FLUFF-DRY CYCLE.

saturday

STOP THE EXECUTION!

....YOU'D BETTER HAVE A GOOD REASON FOR THIS, BOY, OR YOU'RE REALLY GONNA BE IN BIG TROUBLE.
Bill Tucker

GIVE UP PRETTY BOY... YOU AIN'T GOT A CHANCE.

IF I GIVE UP YOU GOTTA SUPPORT ME WITH FOOD STAMPS AND UNEMPLOYMENT CHECKS.

ONLY CHICKEN-HEARTED COWARDS GIVE UP!
Bill Tidwell

tuesday

YOU KNOW WHAT'S WRONG WITH TODAY'S KIDS?... THEY GROW UP WITHOUT HEROES.

...AS A KID I HAD BOLD, COURAGEOUS HEROES... ROBIN HOOD, FLASH GORDON, ZORRO.

DO YOU HAVE ANY HEROES WITH OUTSTANDING QUALITIES, MAGGOT?
MISS SEPTEMBER
Bill Rechin

wednesday

Bill Tidwell

thursday

...COMMANDANT'S WAITING TO SEE YOU.

POULET, YOU BLEW IT AGAIN! YOU'RE A @X!!#! BUBBLEBRAINED BOOB!...YOU AGREE?
YESSIR.

WHAT DID HE WANT?
A SECOND OPINION.

DELICIOUS BEEF STEW... ...I'D LIKE TO COMPLIMENT THE CHEF.
...HE'S OUT BACK PITCHIN' HORSESHOES.

ANYTHING ELSE I CAN TELL YOU, CAPTAIN?
Bill Tochin

TELL ME COWS WEAR HORSESHOES.

saturday

ACCORDING TO OUR MAP THERE'S A TELEGRAPH STATION FOUR THOUSAND MILES DUE EAST.

I HOPE IT'S GOT A RESTROOM
Bill Tekai

GERMS EVERYWHERE!

DO YOU REALIZE GERMS ARE ONE OF MAN'S WORST ENEMIES?

...ONLY THE AUTOMOBILE KILLS MORE PEOPLE.

..THAT'S WHY YOU'LL NEVER FIND AN AUTOMOBILE IN MY STEW.

tuesday

HOW'RE THE MEN DOING IN THE SEX EDUCATION CLASS?
...WE ONLY HAD TWO FAILURES ON THE FINAL EXAM.

...WHAT DID THEY GET WRONG?

THEY MISSPELLED STORK.

wednesday

EVER HAD A TUNE STICK IN YOUR MIND AND YOU CAN'T REMEMBER THE NAME OF IT?

..TRY SINGING A FEW BARS.

OH SAY CAN YOU SEE...
CLANK

thursday

EVER GET TIRED OF DIGGIN' IN THE SAME PLACE DAY AFTER DAY?
KID, I'VE GONE FROM ONE END OF THIS FORT TO THE OTHER ...I'VE SEEN EVERYTHING IT HAS TO OFFER.
Bill Griffith

THE FORT CAN'T OFFER YOU THIS.

CHALK ONE UP FOR THE FORT.

friday

KNOCK KNOCK KNOCK KNOCK
WANNA BUY A DELICIOUS MONGOLIAN PEABIRD?
BOOM!

ALL I KNOW IS, IT'S A BIG FAVORITE ON OUR DINNER TABLE.

saturday

'TEN-SHUN!

CLANK
KLINK
..SHALL I HAVE BRUCE TRY THAT AGAIN, SIR?
Bill Tidwell

I'M AFRAID HIS LEOTARDS WON'T TAKE THE STRAIN.

WHY DID YOU JOIN THE LEGION, BENTLEY?

I ROBBED SIX BANKS AND KILLED FOURTEEN MEN...THE JUDGE WAS GONNA THROW THE BOOK AT ME.

THE LEGION AIN'T EASY, BENTLEY.

NEITHER IS SERVING THIRTY DAYS.

tuesday

WHERE'S THE COMMANDANT?
TAKING HIS PET RAT FOR A WALK...

...THOSE TWO CERTAINLY GET ALONG GREAT.

IT'S THE SON HE NEVER HAD.

wednesday

POWER, POULET...THAT'S WHAT'S IT ALL ABOUT...

...YOU GOTTA FIGHT AND CLAW YOUR WAY TO THE TOP...STEP ON ANYONE WHO GETS IN YOUR WAY.

...IF HE'S THAT HEARTLESS, HOW COME HE ALWAYS SENDS A CHECK TO THE MALARIA FUND?

IT'S MADE OUT TO THE MOSQUITOES.
Ben Rankin

thursday

LEGIONNAIRES ARE MADE OF IRON... LEGIONNAIRES ARE MADE OF STEEL

LEGIONNAIRES ARE MEAN MACHINES..
PLINK.

TAKE COVER!
WHAT'S HE AFRAID OF?
RUST.
Bill Rechin

friday

WHAT A BEAUTIFUL NIGHT
...MUCH TOO NICE TO SIT BEHIND THIS DUMB DUNE...

...THINK I'LL GO FOR A SNEAK.
Bill Tidwell

saturday

DID YOU ENJOY THE CANDLELIGHT DINNER, SIR?

THE SUCKLING PIG WAS UNDISTINGUISHED, ...IT LACKED CHARACTER AND SINCERITY.

YOU'RE SUPPOSED TO EAT THE DANGED THING, NOT GIVE HIM A JOB!
Bill Tidwell

...THE COMMANDANT CHARGES YOU WITH STICKING THE TAIL OF HIS PET RAT IN THE ELECTRIC PENCIL SHARPENER.

ALAS, I REPENT... TAKE MY CONFESSION.

I CAN'T READ THIS.
...YOU EVER TRY WRITING WITH A LIMP RAT?

tuesday

YOU GOT YOUR CHOICE, SCHEMEESE... WE OFFER THE V.I.P. OR THE NO-FRILLS EXECUTION...

...WITH THE V.I.P. YOU GET A PUCCI BLINDFOLD... YOUR CHOICE OF ROPE.... AND SCENTED BULLETS BY FABERGE!
...AND THE NO-FRILLS?
Bill Tedesco

CRAZY FERNANDO, AND HIS SINGING WEEDEATER.

wednesday

WHAT'S THE DELAY? ...I'VE BEEN WAITING FOR TWO HOURS.

THE FIRING SQUAD'S IN CHICAGO.....

...IT'S THE LAST LEG OF THEIR GOOD-WILL TOUR.

thursday

YOU'RE IN LUCK, SCHEMEESE.... THE FIRING SQUAD CAN'T MAKE IT BACK IN TIME.

IS THAT MY PARDON?

...IT'S YOUR RAINCHECK.

AS A FINAL GESTURE, I'D LIKE TO PRESENT THE FIRING SQUAD WITH A BOTTLE OF CHAMPAGNE....
...MAY I SEE THE WINE LIST?

...YOUR PRICES ARE VERY REASONABLE.
Bill Tidwell

IT'S HAPPY HOUR.

saturday

G'MORNING BIRDLEGS.
HI'YA BIRDLEGS
WHAT-A-SAY, BIRDLEGS?

...STICKS AND STONES MAY BREAK MY BONES... BUT WORDS WILL NEVER HURT ME...

HI, BIRDLEGS.
Bill Tenlane

AAGGHHH

tuesday

SIR, THE RATS DIDN'T EAT ALL THE CHEESE....

...COULD WE GIVE IT TO THE MEN FOR THANKSGIVING?

...AND THE NEXT DAY THEY'D WANT CRACKERS.

wednesday

I'D NEVER'VE PICKED YOU FOR THE TYPE TO JOIN THE LEGION, MANCHEZ.
I JOINED TEN YEARS AGO TO GET RID OF MY RACIST ATTITUDE.

...THAT'S A BEAUTIFUL THING TO DO...

THAT'S EASY FOR YOU TO SAY, ...HONKY.
Bill Tucker

thursday

I CAN'T BELIEVE IT'S THANKSGIVING DAY AND WE ONLY GET ONE MORSEL TO EAT

HERE'S YOUR HALF.
YECHT!

WHAT'S WRONG?
I DON'T LIKE MORSEL.

friday

I AIN'T AS DUMB AS YOU SAY
WHAT'S TWO PLUS TWO?

FOUR
IT'S A MIRACLE

...TEEN.

saturday

INSPEC...SHUN!

GRAB

YOU CAN'T INSPECT A CANNON THAT WAY.
YOU TELL HIM.

LOOK HOW PUNY MY FLOWER IS...HOW COME IT WON'T GROW ANY?

STRAIGHTEN UP, FUNGUS-FACE, OR I'LL CRACK YOU BETWEEN THE PODS!
SPOING

IT MUST BE WONDERFUL TO HAVE A GREEN THUMB

tuesday

"CHEW
"CHEW
"CHOMP
CHEW
TODAY COULD BE THE DAY I GET ONE WORD OF KINDNESS.

SPLAT

HE STOPPED! HE'S COMING BACK...I HOPE THIS IS IT.

I WANNA SAY ONE THING...
..NICE CATCH.

wednesday

WHAT ARE YOU IN FOR, MERLE?
CROCK WAS WALKING HIS PET RAT.....

....AND I SAID, "GOOD MORNING, SIR... GOOD MORNING, RAT."

WHAT'S WRONG WITH THAT?
WELL...NORMALLY THE RAT WALKS IN FRONT.
Bill Tedin

thursday

HAS THE COMMANDANT HAD HIS MORNING COFFEE?

SWISH.. HIT.. SWISH.. SWISH
HIT.. HIT
SWISH
Bill Tidwell

...ONE BLACK COFFEE FOR THE COMMANDANT.

friday

saturday

HOW'D YOU LIKE THAT LITTLE GAL I FIXED YOU UP WITH LAST NIGHT.?

BOOM
...I JUST DON'T UNDERSTAND HIM.
IT'S EASY... ONE BOOM MEANS YES... TWO BOOMS MEANS NO.

monday

YOU PUT ON A FEW POUNDS AROUND THE HIPS...HAVEN'T YA?

...I'LL HAVE YOU KNOW I CAN STILL GET INTO MY HIGH SCHOOL PROM OUTFIT.

...EVEN THE MACKINAW AND JACKBOOTS?

tuesday

I'M GETTING WRINKLES!

WRINKLES ARE A SIGN OF MATURITY...
...THE PINNACLE OF ONE'S MENTAL CAPABILITIES
...GUESS I CAN STOP WORRYING ABOUT THESE LAUGH-LINES, EH!?

YOU MEAN CROW'S FEET.

wednesday

I'D LIKE TO CHECK OUT "HOW TO FIGHT YOUR FEARS"... "STOP RUNNING SCARED"... AND "LEARNING TO COPE"

SORRY, THEY'VE ALL BEEN CHECKED OUT.
Bill Tackett

WAAAAAA

thursday

CROCK'S A TYRANT..... WHEN HE SAYS "JUMP"... YOU SAY "HOW HIGH?"

JUMP!
REMEMBER WHAT I TOLD YOU TO SAY.
CROCK'S A TYRANT

WHAT'D I DO WRONG, OTTO?
...LIVED THROUGH YOUR CHILDHOOD DISEASES.

I'VE BEEN TAKING LONG WALKS TO LOSE A FEW POUNDS.
MOMMIE USED TO TAKE ME FOR LONG WALKS.
Bill Watterson

THOSE ARE TIMES YOU ALWAYS CHERISH.

ONLY IF YOU FIND YOUR WAY BACK

saturday

HI, SWEETS, ...WANTA HIT SOME NIGHT SPOTS?

SORRY...BUT I'M GONNA BE DANCING IN THAT BIG BALLROOM UP YONDER

I THOUGHT I KNEW ALL THE SPOTS AROUND HERE.
Bill Tidwell

monday

YOU SURE THIS IS BEEF STEW?

WOULD I LIE TO YOU?

THEN HOW COME I JUST PASSED THE LONE RANGER RIDING A HONDA?

tuesday

PRETTY BOY'S LAYING SIEGE TO OUTPOST FIVE!...ASSEMBLE THE RESCUE SQUAD.

WE'LL BE MARCHING DAY AND NIGHT TO REACH OUTPOST FIVE..... EVERY SECOND COUNTS!
I'M RARING TO GO, SIR.

THEN GO NOW... I DON'T WANT TO BE STOPPING EVERY FIVE MINUTES.

I HEAR CROCK IS PRETTY TOUGH!
...WE'RE TREATED LIKE DOGS!

I CAN TAKE IT!

...YOU EVER BEEN CURBED ON A HOT SAND DUNE?

MORE FUN FOR THE LEGIONS OF CROCK FANS

CROCK	1-3868-2	$1.25

AND FROM THE WIZARD OF ID:

I'M OFF TO SEE THE WIZARD	1-3700-7	$1.25
LONG LIVE THE KING	1-3655-8	$1.25
THE PEASANTS ARE REVOLTING	1-3671-X	$1.25
THERE'S A FLY IN MY SWILL	1-3687-6	$1.25
WE'VE GOT TO STOP MEETING LIKE THIS	1-3633-7	$1.25

Send to: FAWCETT BOOKS GROUP
Mail Order Dept., 1 Fawcett Place
P.O. Box 1014, Greenwich, Conn. 06830

NAME _____

ADDRESS _____

CITY _____

STATE _____ ZIP _____

I enclose $_____, which includes total price of all books ordered plus 60¢ for book postage and handling for the first book and 25¢ for each additional. If my order is for five books or more, I understand that Fawcett will pay all postage and handling.